BENEATH THE SOUTHERN CRUX

Marilyn Zelke Windau

I0390031

WATER'S EDGE PRESS
TUCSON, AZ

Copyright © 2023 by Marilyn Zelke Windau

All rights reserved.

Printed in the United States of America

Water's Edge Press LLC
Tucson, AZ
watersedgepress.com

ISBN: 978-1-952526-12-1

Credits

Cover design by Water's Edge Press
Images licensed through iStock

A Water's Edge Press First Edition

Also by Marilyn Zelke Windau

Adventures in Paradise, Finishing Line Press, 2014
Momentary Ordinary, Pebblebrook Press, 2014
Owning Shadows, Kelsay Books, 2017
Hiccups Haunt Wilson Avenue, Kelsay Books, 2018

Author's Note

I was nine years old when Queen Elizabeth visited Chicago. She and Prince Phillip had come from England to declare the St. Lawrence Seaway officially open. They disembarked at Navy Pier from their ship's tender to walk a red-carpeted path to the International Trade Fair, the initial stop on their tour of the city.

My mother had taken my brother, sister, and me to see the queen and to visit the fair. It was a day of wonder for me: first seeing people from all over the world in their colorful native dress, hearing a multitude of new languages, watching dances to unique music, tasting never-before tried foods. Then, because I was a young girl in love with the fairytales of "Sleeping Beauty," "Snow White," and "Cinderella," to see royalty—a queen especially—was a dream come true. She had traveled across a sea!

From that day forward, I longed to travel and have been fortunate to have journeyed to many lands.

Beneath the Southern Crux gives insight into three such journeys. "Around the Horn," "Over the Andes," and "Down Under," the three sections of the book, recount trips taken with my husband in 2014, 2015, and 2020.

Like the native peoples who found and settled lands below the equator as well as the Portuguese and Italians who explored there long ago, we, as travelers, also sought the stars of the southern cross to center us and guide us to our destinations.

Just as early explorers and ancient peoples created stories about this starry gift of the night, I offer you these poems inspired beneath the Southern Crux.

In thanks to and recognition of my life travel companions:

my "See America First" parents, my worldwide, adventure-seeking friends, and my husband and family, ever ready to explore new places and cultures.

Acknowledgements

The author is grateful to the editors of the following publications in which these poems first appeared, some in different form:

The Water Poems (Water's Edge Press, 2017): "Bergie Bits"

Wisconsin Fellowship of Poets Calendar, 2020: "In the Sacred Valley of Peru"

Around the Horn

Orion on Vacation 1
Tango 2
Ship Horn 3
Storm at Sea 4
River in the Sea 5
Seal Lords of Deception 6
Albatross 8
Bergie Bits 9
Antarctica 10
A Chilean Cemetery 12
Dog in the Doorway 14
Hanuxa apaernix 15
Recognition of Origin 16
Rain! 17

Over the Andes

In the Land of Crumpled Paper 21
The White City 22
On the road: Arequipa to Chivay, Peru 23
Waiting in the Cold 24
Content 26
Delicious! 27
Machu Picchu Repose 28
Vicuna 29
El Dia de Miguel 30
Colca Canyon, Central Andes, Peru 32
Nazca Geoglyphs 33
In the Sacred Valley of Peru 34

Difference in Belief 35
Lake Titicaca 36
Mostly Barefoot from Birth 37
6:28 a.m., Saturday, March 14, 2015 38
Quindio 40
Rain in the Jungle 41
Use your imagination 42

Down Under

Wavelets 47
Ocean Arrogance 48
Sea Breathe 49
Oh! To Watch the Sea! 50
Cruising the Cascades 51
Genius! 52
A Māori Legend 53
Proboscis Promise 54
The Haka Dance 55
It's Not What You Think 56
Follow the Silver 57
Maungami, Caught by the Sun 58
Māori Elder's Wake 59
Old Retold 60
Baa 61
Mysterious Bean 62
Rotorua's Ring of Fire Restaurant and Spa 63
Locks of Love 64
A Binky of Hope 65

AROUND THE HORN

Orion on Vacation

Ok, the rest of the world is watching
"Dancing with the Stars."
The rest of the world doesn't know
that Orion—that constellation
that's been fighting battles for centuries,
is doing somersaults in Argentina.

It's February.
He's upside down,
doing cartwheels.
It's summer.
What's not to love?

His sword swings in celebration,
not in threat.
His stance is one of fun.

This is a new Orion for me.
He was always a stalwart hero.
He guarded, protected
centuries of citizens.

Now that I think about it,
he deserves a break,
a rest, a time out,
a vacation down south.
He can be back on guard
up north in fall.

Tango

When you talk tango,
you talk prostitutes
on the street
displaying their wares.

When you talk tango,
you talk men, in response,
showing off their thighs,
their tight pants' prowess.

Dancers, looking for more,
took their routine to Europe.
Those of upscale refrained,
denied the base-low origins.
Modifying moves,
steps were applauded.

Tango: the throwing
of the female partner,
in a show of dominance,
the lip thrust,
the hip hold,
the kick by she,
which he counters,
to whisk her out
in a long trail gown,
moving perhaps
toward equality.

Ship Horn

It's a C note,
an octave down alto.
It moans and alarms
any and all small craft
who navigate home in this fog.

Dolphins, invigorated by reverberations,
lace-scallop the ocean surface,
make hills of themselves,
humorous humps of surprise.

A fishing trawler takes note
of pumped sound,
hears volume, not distance.
Very late, it sees the wall of vessel,
swings hard to port and safety.

Salmon jostle in the hold below,
rub silver skin of kin,
flick and flap arched trapezoidal tails,
yearn for wet
and current
and silence.

Storm at Sea

Winter/summer droplets
tail-trail the window,
like sperm,
frantically seeking home.
A swirl, a sweep,
a dance in unison
of hundreds out there
in the storm.
Their comet tails train
westward, then southward.
They slash the way
of the prevailing winds
to rein in at sill
unfulfilled,
to await their brothers
streaming over them,
furious in pursuit.

River in the Sea

    South of the Falkland Islands

Within the undulating
sway grass-bound banks,
the sea shivers its current forward,
widens to the horizon's plates
where cumulus accumulates.
Reflected light security-blankets
a hidden populace of icefish,
of dolphin, of whales.
Deep on the Antarctic storage shelf
rocks are silent.
Salt murmurs the water,
quieting icemaker desires.
Glitter funnels toward me,
spews shine,
sparkle dust.

Seal Lords of Deception

They sit, sunning themselves
on the rocks of Deception Island,
deep in the bottom seas of the earth.
There, they think themselves kings
of this land, Antarctica.

Harems of girlie-seals flap flippers,
twist and shout their necks and voices,
chitchat while glancing diagonally
above them.

The kings seek the highest levels.
They lord it over all mistresses
and all pretenders to their thrones.

Basking in their fat, blubberous ways,
they sway rhythmically
right to left, up and down.
They are content to receive homage.

If, perchance, a young upstart
starts up, they grin.
They relish a challenge
to their thrones, to their prowess.

Females secretly take sides.
Cute and coy, they privately cheer
the younger, the older.
They await the outcome
of the flapping, the biting,
the wounding, the blood in the sea.

They cuddle their young,
swim and fish, knowing
they are protected, if not respected.

It seems they realize, coldly,
that survival is of the fittest.

Albatross

White the tutu
of this ballerina,
her arms in soft angles bent.
She dances with no legs,
no *pas de deux*.
She careens the wind,
slices with stropped sharpness—
as if through creamed butter,
as if through meringue.
She rises in crescendo.
She dips and floats
extending her grace forward
on silent flow of dream air.

Bergie Bits

> British expression for small parts of icebergs

Thousands of white pupils
bulge skyward in blue-grey eye pools,
bob-float the waters of the Amalia Glacier.
They vibrate ripples of lesser vision
than their stalwart valley mother seer
on shore.

These bergie bits, born as calves,
no longer nurse or moo.
They fizzle cold salt,
cavort our wake,
somersault the sea.

Antarctica

At the bottom of the earth
when you find your senses,
you see ice glacier blue—
a condensed color
created by snow's pressure,
but brighter than Roman sea glass—
colder. There is a nose, a salt sense,
a reckoning of whale, humpback,
of seal, leopard,
of dolphin, hourglass,
of albatross, black-browed,
careening, arching,
balleting their space.

We are interlopers,
invaders of a realm
not meant for our habitation.
We come to learn,
to glory in magnificence.

Truths are told in trials,
in struggles for the pole,
in treaties to extend purity
to this planet region,
in hope of species' gifts,
taken from them, not offered,
in quiet, cold lagoons.

Icebergs, born of glacial,
European-named mothers,
calve themselves into the sea.
They break apart, somersault
with the wake of ships,
fizz in turning heads and minds.

And so, we and they float en masse,
understanding, in awe and shock
of temperature, of desolation,
of how.

A Chilean Cemetery

You knew the way
but graciously walked at my right knee
for many blocks of Punta Arenas.
We passed other dogs,
who peered and leered,
who tried to get a rise from you
with no response.
You were on a mission,
truly, a mission.

Good white dog, you led us
without directing, to the city cemetery
with its tall, sun-bleached guardian walls,
comforting in their arms of hold me,
hold them.

The marble slab at entry was your sanctuary.
There, you laid your short-haired body down.
You cocked your ears to hear angel voices,
as you exhaled on cool stone,
found peace and comfort
on that same cool stone
which held your city's loved ones.

Small houses are their eternal homes,
architectural, above ground wonders,
complete with columns and fences,
metal-welded flowers and archways.
Vision-narrowing, long pathways
lined with huge pruned cypress trees
gave pause to a soft forever.

You, our guide, were no longer there
when we emerged from the quiet.
Your duty done, you had ambled
from siesta back to city.

Dog in the Doorway

From half a block down
I could see only
his black hind end.
His thin pointed whip tail
was arc-raised toward the lintel beam.
Long, strong legs braced a stance
which could have won best in show.
Gaining his doorway, I learned
the subject of his rapt attention:
tents!

A hostelería in Castro, Isla de Chiloe,
had rented their atrium
to young, backpacked travelers.
Puffs of red and khaki and green
huddle-hilled our down-the-corridor view.
His smooth narrow nose turned,
forced fur-fringed, upright ears
to command attention.
Golden head-lamped eyes seemed to ask,
"Con permiso?"
La turista in me said, "Si! Vamos!"
Trotting ahead, he turned,
dipped his head in gracias.

Hanuxa apaernix

> Moon and Stars

In my tierra del fuego,
my land of fire,
in my language Yaghan,
I reach back hundreds
of your time ages.

We do not keep these years,
more than three hundred of them,
you say to me, you Spaniards,
who came into our birthplace.

My people seek the coolness
of the moon and points of night—
light to contrast the heat of sun's fire.

White beams, white sheets,
white stars speckle-dot our brows.
Evenings bring stories of ago.

I remember and I speak.
I am the last to voice my language.
Hear me now.

Ah, only the moon and stars listen.

Recognition of Origin

It's hidden
until recognized
in rolled rrr's
of a language
of the south,
given by the east.

It's hidden
until recognized
in the rounded muscles
of sculptured mothers,
clinging to shawls
and children,
whose eyes are wide open
as their madres blink.

It's hidden
in Ayssen's twin mountains,
one white-capped in snow,
one blackened in rock face.
The earth proves
the truth of eon-long defiance.

In this age, there is no hiding.
The rrr's and the round madres,
the mountains and the lakes
of emerald
portend life in pesos.
They forego the moments
of yearn and ritual
and remembrance of their origin.

Rain!

We await a cloud,
one cloud,
a solitary cloud
on our western horizon.

So rare a sighting it is
that we dance and sing.
Our rain sticks voice the waters
from the sky.
We tip them slowly
so that the gods will hear us.
We want the rain that comes
to be long and steady.

We are forever hopeful
in this most arid region of Chile.

Our ancestors, the Mapuche people,
taught us to cut stems of cacti,
to let the lengths dry,
to scoop up the prickers
and push them back in.

We created an inner spiral of clickers,
covered the ends of the cactus tube—
but not before we added seeds
and small bits of stones.

We use these idiophones,
these instruments of music,
to coerce the gods of rain,
to woo them into flirting
their moisture with our earth,
for our crops,
for our survival.

OVER THE ANDES

In the Land of Crumpled Paper

The earth made it difficult for you, didn't it, Peru?
You are a land that the gods took up in their hands
and crumpled like paper,
creating those three Incan stair steps you so cherish:

the upper world, the universe,
governed by the condor,
of ever-watchful flight, of spirit

the middle universe, the earth,
governed by the puma,
of power, of men, ever hungry,
planting corn and beans,
in each returning season,
on every rock-secured terrace

and the lower universe, the core,
aided by the serpent,
the snake of wisdom, of learning,
to whom all of earth return
to the energy of the universe.

You, Peru, of upthrusts, of canyons,
of seashore cliffs and plateaus.
You, of cold and snow,
of hot and rain,
of height and depth,
mountains and jungles,
you are a land worthy of glory.

Your people, since early times,
Moche and Nazca, Uros and Wari,
learned from, leaned on the land,
perfected life and honor
to those that gave you life.

The White City

Who named you?

Was it the Aymara people,
who were in awe of El Misti,
the volcanic mountain,
there in the distance,
towering above them?

It is said they settled at its feet,
naming their city "Are" (summit)
"Quipa" (lies beyond).

Or was it the fourth Inca emperor,
Mayta Capac?
He saw fertile land,
recognized its imposing position
between his city, Cusco, and the ocean.
Did he voice in his Quechua tongue:
"Ari qhipay—let's stay here."

The Spaniards kept that name in 1540.
They mined El Misti's sillar,
soft, white volcanic stone.
Light in weight and impervious to water,
they erected white churches,
white government buildings.

An 1800's earthquake devastated that Arequipa,
but the White City remains today,
rebuilt upon the rubble.
Now a UNESCO Heritage site, it glows.

On the road: Arequipa to Chivay, Peru

We wind upward to the sun,
pass pink Judah rock hills
where prickly verde arms and fingers
stretch their cacti presence.

Pink changes to white—
the eons-old white lava given
by mountains, the volcanoes
of the god family:
Padre Misti, Madre Chacani,
and baby Picchu Picchu.

The ichu grasses replace cacti
at 3,500 meters altitude.
Their blades cut the thin air,
slice oxygen into small portions,
dare the newcomer to walk faster,
breathe deeper, steady consciousness.

Soon the grasses give way
to sun-paled, rumple-bumply puff mosses.
Yareta's bulls eyes circle-dot the earth,
grow only a miniscule yearly.

We reach the top of the world—
the highest point on our road journey:
all rock and snow and wind.

I stack five stones,
repeat an ancient people's offering
of thanks and well wishes
to their protective volcano god family.

Waiting in the Cold

There at the top of their world,
there with the condor, the Incan sky god,
Peruvian women wait.

They shiver their dark braided hair,
their earth-colored skin,
their torsos draped in woolen shawls,
not alpaca.

Alpaca is for the customers.
These women have wares to sell,
at 13,000 feet in Andes' altitude.

A turn-out on a highway,
they invest their lives, their living,
on people who are not their own.

Those people on the bus
transcend vehicles,
emerge into another culture,
with thoughts of a buying spree.

The French woman hopes for thanks from a cousin.
The German knows his uncle will like this hat.

The Andean woman pulls blue plastic tarps
across a space in time,
a space to reveal history, culture.
The cold bites her hands, her spirit.
The baby alpaca feels cool to her touch.

The man wants the hat for three dollars.
What is fair trade to those who don't deal
in other peoples' worlds?

Snow is falling,
wet snow, sleet.
The winds from the mountains
give knowledge of the past.
The Andean women pull blue plastic forward
to cover their hand wrought valuables.

What is the price for heritage,
for history, for life now?

Content

Outside a restaurant in Chivay,
the short-haired yellow dog
gazes furtively up at you
and away,
brings her head and brown eyes
down shyly, yet hopefully.

"Hola, perro," you say.
Orbs raise, blink.
Tail wags, thumping the stucco wall
where you lean.
"Oh, you're a good dog.
You're such a good dog."

She sits, raises her paw,
presses your leg with kindness in return.

Confirming friendship,
she settles down, rests her chin
on your shoe,
content to be near you and rest.

Delicious!

They call it "manjar blanco."
White and creamy, it is spread
on cakes, cookies, pies,
on breakfast rolls.
It is a Peruvian delight.

Every day across the country,
cooks are creating this wonder.
They place a small can
of sweetened, condensed milk
into a slightly-covered pan of water,
set it on the stove, and turn on the heat.
The unopened can is simmered
for three hours!

When removed and opened,
"manjar blanco" is revealed,
thick and gooey,
ready to be gifted to pastries.
It means "delicacy."
It means "delicious!"

Machu Picchu Repose

Ah, Pachacuti, you have come for a visit.
We are prepared to greet, to honor you
and all your entourage.
We will gather maize of black and blue.
of red and yellow.
We will pull the quinoa,
butcher alpacas, roast them
and sauce them.

We will assemble our young women,
those who will be honored to serve,
to show joy at their choosing.

The trapezoidal stone niches will be alight
with welcoming fire, comfort light
in the darkness of stone rooms.

Go out, Lord!
See the brilliance of the heavens!
The stars are aligned in your greatness.

Enjoy your repose with us
here, at the top of the world,
close to the condor's realm.

We have toiled to please you.
We have lowered mountains,
created inns of relaxation,
tiered the earth to provide sustenance.

The road to this place is guided
by a pathway of constellations,
the Crux,
protected by your infinite power,
you, our Incan emperor.

Vicuna

So tiny, this camelid
has fleece softer than silk.
Protected by the government
of Peru, it is shorn only
by approved resident farmers.

Wild ancestors of alpacas,
vicunas appear shy.
They meander the Andes
at highest elevations,
graze greenery during the day,
return nightly to favored places,
kick up their hooves joyfully.

Tourists who obtain the fuzzy yarn,
soft scarves, socks, sweaters
are grateful and lucky buyers.
Rare purchases, these,
as historically, only the Incan emperor
and his nobility were allowed
clothing made from this fiber.
Anyone else faced sure death.

Vicunas are golden,
in more ways than one,
the revered animal of Peru.

El Día de Miguel

Miguel threw off his striped woven blanket as the sun's first rays invaded the crack in the doorway curtain. Time for work, he dressed quickly, took coffee from his wife, a round loaf, and a stubby banana, as well as a separate bag for midday almuerzo.

Pedro, his burro, was busy tearing grass chews from the adobe house's small front yard.

"Vamos," said Miguel as he untied Pedro's rope tether from a wooden stake. He burdened his friend with bags of tools, water, and food.

The sun warmed the terraces for three hours as they climbed past them, counting the steps to the top of the mountain. At last, at 3,500 meters, they turned to look.

Potatoes flowered purple. Lima beans set pods. Spears of tall quinoa flamed red grain. Prickly pear cacti bumped ovoid yellow-green fruit on their nopales' edges.

Rainclouds were forming on the far side of Picchu Picchu. A few more hours and it would be wet—hard to work.

Miguel pulled his wood-handled hoe from one of Pedro's packs, tossed the other packs to the earth. Happy to be free, Pedro sought the choicest of the mountain-irrigated greens, then blink-closed his eyes.

Miguel grabbed the two handles of his hoe, pressed the steel blade into soil. His Incan ancestors had used bronze blades that required constant sharpening. Back and forth he rocked as he dug, arching weeds over his shoulder.

Stopping only to wipe his brow or reposition his brimmed hat to match the sun's position, he worked continuously for five hours. Then he moved down to the next terrace, ate his meager almuerzo of empanadas and manzanos.

The best for last, he pulled dry koka leaves from his pocket purse, folded each in half, tore out seam stems. When he had fifty, he folded them together, stuffed them in his left cheek, sipped water, and then chewed.

Back and forth, as he had done with his hoe, he moved the mash across his tongue to the other cheek. Soon the tingling began. Soon his energy returned.

Always more tasks for tomorrow, Miguel weeded for two more hours before whistling to Pedro and loading packs for the easier downward journey home.

Before gathering in his friend's rope, he knelt, grasped soil to his palms, raised his hands to Pachamama, mother universe, and gave thanks.

Then he lowered the hands which held the abundance of his life, and gave thanks to the mountain, to Picchu Picchu, before starting his descent.

Midway back, the rains came. The thunder god boomed his power, shot his bolts of light to earth.

Clearing somewhat, the rainbow god appeared. Miguel knew to bow his head, hold his hand over his mouth. That god would take his teeth, he had learned at a young age, if he looked at the arc of colors.

Teresa was waiting at her cook pots when he returned. Miguel could smell the sheep head soup. Pedro gulped water from his leather bucket as Miguel tied his tether back to the wooden stake and removed the heavy packs.

El sol oranged the skies as Teresa, Miguel, Maria, Tomas, Elena, and little Alejandro sank into their reed-straw mattress beds, pulled up soft blankets of alpaca, and dreamed of tomorrow's dawn.

Colca Canyon, Central Andes, Peru

The mountain side is woven in tabby—
a weft of dark green and yellow green
in row repetition,
in terrace repetition:
Inca garden tapestries.

Nazca Geoglyphs

Some 250 miles south of Lima, Peru
there are pictures drawn into desert earth.
Some say ancient astronauts created these artworks.
Most agree that the Nazca native people dug them
between 500BCE and 500CE

Hummingbird, spider, fish, condor.
Heron, monkey, lizard.
Dog, cat, tree, flower.
Human!

Were they made for the gods in the heavens to admire?
Were they made in thanks?
Were they fertility symbols?
Were they shallow troughs to transport
the little rainfall received?

Scraping away reddish-brown pebbles
exposed light-colored clay,
making visible the line designs.
Lime in the clay earth and morning moisture
hardened and protected the pictures.

Some say Nazca people walked
these picture paths, praying for rain,
while their families sang
above them on hillsides.
Survival promotes creativity.

In the Sacred Valley of Peru

After the war between the plates:
the American and the Nazca—
after the pushing and shoving was done—
the thrusting of up and over,
down and under,
someone draped a velvet blanket
of moss green on the mountains
and let them sleep.

Difference in Belief

We Spaniards in our wisdom
have eight hundred forty-two saints,
whose tears and bones are kept in glass-cased boxes
in Madrid, in Rome, in Mexico City, in Cusco.
We know. We claimed the world for Christ.

We, the tribes of Moche, Nazca, and Wari,
knew before they came.
We knew the earth, the clay,
the techniques of stirrup pottery,
the decoration of the three levels of the universe.

We knew the condor, the puma, and the snake—
levels of existence which kept us whole,
reverent, and in whose praise,
we gained quinoa, corn, beans, potatoes,
sustenance.

We gave our wisdom to Incan kings.
Their strength failed them when the Spaniards came
thundering on horseback with swords of steel,
with diseases unknown to us.

The Inca rulers relinquished their puma-earth power,
succumbed to the Genesis snake, to illness,
to new rulers, unlike our own.

We still look up, we the people of the Andes.
We look to the mountains.
We look to the sun.
We look to the constellations of the southern crux
in whose path our cities are delineated.
We live on toward our future,
assured by the trail of our past.

Lake Titicaca

Oh, you mountain gods, you Apus!
We did not obey your command
to not climb the highest Andes mountain.
We wished to see your sacred fires there.

The devil tempted us, persuaded us.
We left our beautiful valley
to walk upwards.

The pumas! You sent the pumas
to destroy us—all but two.

Seeing this slaughter,
the sun god in despair
cried for forty days
and forty nights.

His tears of sadness created this lake.
Its flooding waters transformed
the mountain lions to stone.

We named you:
"titi" for the pumas
"kaka" for stone.
You are Lake Titicaca,
lake of the stone pumas.

Mostly Barefoot from Birth

The Peruvian Uros people have foot-swayed softly
on their waterbed-like islands for thousands of years.
Shoes are not needed for their everyday life.

They must have shoes somewhere,
hidden though,
unimportant as they are
on the floating reed platforms they call home.

Perhaps only the president of each island has a pair
for when some supply is needed from Puno.
He pulls them out
from under a handwoven blanket
in a corner of his hollow reed house,
boards the village reed boat,
paddles Lake Titicaca to the city.
Then, only then, does he slide them on his feet,
feet that have been mostly bare since birth.

6:28 a.m., Saturday, March 14, 2015

    Along the Tambopata River, Peru

Twenty-three dusky head, green parakeets
diamond-shape the sky.
Flying in unison, they swish-scrub air.
They move as a planar shield,
eyes intent for predators.

Singly, they drop to treetops,
to vertically columnize vines,
breaking the diamond into facets.

Green on green, not to be seen,
they wait in stillness.

One lone bird, the sentinel, the lookout,
chooses the victim perch.
Visible, vulnerable atop a sprawling tree-hill of foliage,
he watches, turns,
watches, waits.

With an unknown signal to his flock,
he gives the "all free!"

One first, then four more
fly green to the orange-red cliff slope.

The ritual of pecking begins,
the eating of salt clay,
necessary to detoxify the effects
of the poisonous seed pods of their diet.
From a vantage point far away and above them,
we observe this communal event,
this comradery,
this protective genre scene.

Quickly, it is gone.

The parakeets, as if by whisper-message,
ascend skyward,
reassume their diamond shape,
that of their starry nighttime Southern Cross,
then wing silently away.

Quindío

Oh! How tall you are!
I was 5'8" in 8th grade.
I hovered above most of my classmates.
Dance lessons in gym class
with short boys were not fun.

You, Quindío Wax Palm,
are the tallest palm tree in the world.
You, of the tropics of northern Peru,
are my predecessor.

So many animals seek you for shelter.
You don't dance with them.
You provide them with safety.

A yellow-eyed parrot relies on you
for its habitat.
It has nowhere else to go.
Endangered as it is,
you, wax palm, provide its survival.

I was so short in comparison to you.
My 5'8" compared to your 200 feet!
No parrot would seek me out.
I'm glad they found you.
I'm glad the boys I knew grew.

Rain in the Jungle

Midday rain pummels the Amazon earth,
forms pumpkin-soup puddles,
fills entry tunnels to leaf-cutter ants'
subterranean homes.
Squirrel monkeys quit their dive-leaps
from tree to tree,
find broad banana leaves for shelter.

Men take shelter in palm-roofed huts,
shake umbrellas, peel clothing,
swish rain tributaries from limbs, from hair.

Capybara mothers take their babies
to the steep grey clay shores
of the Tambopata River
for swim tests and sliding fun.

The anacondas, piranhas, and river otters
revel in this wet environment.
Their eyes are not blurred by rain tears.
This is their element.
Secure, they salivate their hunger.

Use your imagination

From the beginning, he dreamed in stories.
He would wake up on his palette of reed grass
in a fury of thoughts.
He knew his grandmother's tales,
but in the night, in his sleep,
he embellished them into plots
which grabbed him from slumber.
He thought it an illness,
went finally to the shaman,
asked her, "What can I do about this plight?"

The wise woman said to him,
"You must use your imagination. It is a gift."
"But how can I use it? I have no tools," he said.

"Ah," she said. "Do you not go to the river to seek fish?
Let the waters flow your thoughts into speech.
Speak your stories. Repeat your stories.
Those that understand their value will remember."

"Take the yellow and red ochre of our clay.
Take the kohl of our firesticks, cooled from embers.
Use them to make marks, pictures of your thoughts.
Draw on the walls of the high terrace caves,
on the skins of our animal gifts from hunt.
Hang them for all to see."

"Drop-spindle the hair of your alpacas.
Use the skin of onions, cochineal,
indigo to dye it.
Weave the powers of our universe—
the condor, the puma, the snake—
in cloth symbol stories.

Wear this garment proudly and in their honor."

"Go down to the river, scoop the mud of the banks.
Form vessels. Incise your stories there
in the wet of our mother earth.
She will help you to help all recall
and reply the meaning."

"Use your imagination. It is not a plight.
It is a gift. Offer it graciously to our people.
It will be remembered."

DOWN UNDER

Wavelets

Look at you!
Look at you!

You roll out, one after another.
You are family: a son, a daughter.
Again and again, you tuck and curl,
all amniotic fluid,
all foam and spume.
You present at birth a continuum.
Your height is recorded
in ocean meters.
You bump each other,
slap and cavort in fun.

You kids!
I recognize your antics.
Be calm.
Take a nap.
Smooth that blue binky over you.
Don't toss and turn,
just dream
of dolphins and seals and fish and penguins
as playmates, as comrades, as classmates
to sea, and be seen.

Ocean Arrogance

    Outside of Sydney, Australia's harbor, bound for New Zealand

Whoosh. Whine. Whoosh.
You are singing to me
through a crack in the door—
telling me of your presence.

The rocking and swaying aren't enough?
Isn't a clue?

White foam gossip is planely going on
outside my porthole.

I hear your bubble-wash conversations.

Smack me again with a funny
against my bow.

Hit me sternly astern.

I'm ready.

I love your wild talk, your windy dialogue.

We can wave through,
wave together throughout the night.

Sea Breathe

You exhale sheets of white breath,
lungfuls of oxygen
from belly-intake swells.
You count one, two, three, four,
and up to six
then hold
before relinquishing purity
to the foam-washed ocean surface.

Few know this.
Few see your labors,
hear your continuum.
Grateful are those
who join in your pattern,
your rhythm,
your sequence of life.

Oh! To Watch the Sea!

    Off North Cape, New Zealand

A white bird is captured by black of wave,
restored to flight by blue.
Father sky blesses mother earth with sun's rays,
glistening blessings upon her waters,
upon their sons—
the tall forests and the gentle winds.
Fish leap with open mouths,
capture diamonds of light.
I sit and gaze in awe
the striations of white set on the sea,
the infinite sea,
the timeless, endless sea
and hope that my being is united
in its forever.

Cruising the Cascades

> Milford Sound, Doubtful Sound, Dusky Sound
> —South Island, New Zealand

In winter, you don a cloak of snow—
a white wrap over your head.
But this is summer in the southern hemisphere
and you've abandoned that coat.

Today as I meet you in Milford Sound,
you've thrown a boa around your shoulders.
Fluffy with mist, it cloud-floats.

As we cruise by, you peek out of dewy air,
show me your blue side.
Without warning, you quickly change
to wear a moss green dress.
I could liken you to a model—
so erect is your posture.

Your mountain mates,
communal climbs of glacial upbringing,
stand tall, elegant.
We nod and smile in homage to your age,
your strength, your beauty,
your permanence.

Genius!

There is a gift that is sparked by observation,
that is born of creativity.
It's a gift of the realization of possibility.
It's an answer to the question
"For what can I use this to make my life better?"
Our environment provides elements to inspire us.
Intense thought and experiment sustain us.

The Māoris of Aotearoa,
the land of the long white cloud,
found native flax plants.
They gathered the long leaves,
layered and rolled them tightly,
one after another.
They created canoe-like vessels from these rolls,
wove sails from the fronds,
made ropes from the strong fibers,
fashioned skirts for clothing,
bags for cooking in thermal steam holes.

The Pakeha* would say brilliant!
I say genius!

*a New Zealander of European descent

A Māori Legend

Howling. I hear you howling your wind.
You're angry with me, your brother,
for separating the space of love
between our mother, earth,
and our father, sky.

I pushed my feet and arms against them
needing us to be born.
Sunlight touched us.
We became gods.

I am of the forests and people,
and I am guilty!
You will protest me forever
as the god of storms and lightning,
strength and force.

You will create tsunamis, tornadoes,
cyclones, and hurricanes.

I will nurture life in tall trees,
in strong tribes, in unity of humanity.

Let us seek peace, my brother.
We can work together in harmony.
Be gentle with your breath.
Exhale slowly.

Proboscis Promise

New Zealand's Māori people
touch noses in greeting,
based on their belief
that by doing so,
they exchange
a continuous breath of life.

Bird, insect, fish, animal, human—
all share the earth's elements:
water, soil, air.

The Māori seek life, guard life,
and its benefactors.
Nose touching embraces unity
of matter and spirit
with warmth.

The Haka Dance

Chased by enemy tribesmen,
Te Rauparaha ran for his life.
A woman with wild black hair
saw his plight, hid him
in a dark food storage pit,
sat down upon its cover.

"No, I have seen no one,"
she told the band of killers.
"My man is abroad
hunting the flightless moa."

After they were gone,
the woman stood, opened the pit.

The warrior emerged
dancing and shouting.
"Ka mate, ka mate! Ka ora, ka ora!"
I might die! I might die!
I might live! I might live!
"A upane, ka upane, whiti te ra! hi!"
A step upward, another.
The sun shines! Rise!

He thrust out his tongue.
He slapped his tattooed chest and thighs,
stomped his feet violently.
His eyes bulged far
as if to shoot them out of his head.
He waved his weapons wildly
as he chanted his tribal pride,
his newfound strength.

The haka dance was born!
Life had triumphed over death.

It's Not What You Think

Poi.
I know it as goo from Polynesia,
made by boiling, then squooshing taro tubers
into a purplish paste.
Served as a side dish,
it is loved by some, disdained by others.

Poi.
To a Māori woman in Aotearoa,
poi are sacred tools of family, of unity.
Poi are soft white fiber balls,
strung one on each end of a tasseled red rope.
They are swung and twirled in rhythmic circles
as women move,
gyrate hips, shoulders,
thrust arms, pound feet in dance.

Poi energize,
expose femininity,
sensuality, tribal community.

They are global orbs of life
extended.

Follow the Silver

Oh, my son, this is the ponga!
See how tall it is!
Soon your bare feet will be able to climb it,
to gather its treasure from ten meters up.
I will go now and throw down its fronds.
Gather them for me as they fall.
I will teach you of their good will to us.

Father, these look like river ferns,
but they are so much larger.
Silver! They have silver on the stems!

Turn the frond over, my son.
It is rich in shininess.

This night, with little light from our moon,
these fronds will guide us back to home.
We will spread them on our path
as we venture to gather food for our women.
With our arms loaded, we must only glance down.
We will follow the silver.
Ponga's ferns will mark the way
to our journey's end, our safe return.

Maungami, Caught by the Sun

I see you there
hovering in the swirl of the mist
of your deep forest home.

Please, Patupaiarehe, you red-haired fairy,
I, Maungami, humbly request your help.

I love a woman.
She does not love me.
I cannot go on.
I seek death.
I implore you to help me cross over.

Ah, but too late I have asked.
We were nearly across.
You had to leave me.
Dawn came seeking you with its fatal rays.
Now I must stay forever trapped in rock,
as this new mountain.

Māori Elder's Wake

I will sleep here with my brothers
on the floor beneath your bier, O Great One.
You are gone now.
The fairies have crossed you over
to your peace.

For three nights let your wisdom come to us.
Give us your knowledge and your insight.

With respect to you, ancestral elder,
deem us worthy vessels for your gifts.
We will grow stronger nocturnally,
become richer, valued members of our tribe.
Our thanks will be to you.

Old Retold

There are molecules floating in the night sky
in the space between stars.
They are your grandfather, your uncle—
all those who have passed history forward to you,
in the now, in the know.

These molecules of your ancients are reconfigured,
dispersed to the beyond, to the heavens,
or what your ancestors called heavens.

They have complete knowledge:
all the words in all the books
in all the eons of time.
Think of it!

They know the bedtime stories,
the myths, the poems of nature,
the tragedies and comedies of old.

They pass these words on to you in your sleep
so that you can reiterate them in kind
to your kin, to your children, who will remember.

They may not recall the plot or the night
but they will remember the cast, the emotion.
Fear or delight will stun them in years to come.

The words of stories you tell to them—
you may think they're your own.
Perhaps your father set them
in your dreaming subconscious
as new thoughts, as molecules of old
retold.

Baa

As the new queen of the Māori's Aotearoa,
you had us brought here from Australia.
You said, "Let us make of New Zealand a huge farm!"

Oh, Victoria,
millions of my lambs roam the hills,
the mountain slopes, seeking grass.

Did you not bring to this land the red deer also?
The red deer eat all the green of the hillsides.
They cause the rains to erode the land and our food.

Can they not have a new home?
We cannot both survive.

Our wool gives you comfort and warmth.
We are kind and gentle providers.
We do not disturb the flightless kiwi birds
from their burrows.
They do not fear our presence.

We are foreigners, like you.
We wish to settle in peaceably.
The Māori named us "hipi."
Our voice is not threatening.
"Baa" beseeches.

"Baa" seeks harmony.

Mysterious Bean

What does it mean
to discover half a green bean
on the staircase of the Civic Square
in Wellington, New Zealand?

Is it a capital offense to litter produce
or does it promote production
of more crops of greenery?

Is it an omen of scarcity to come—
a waste not/want not moral?

Is it a symbol of abundance—
an item of sharing nature with nature?

Surely a bird or a squirrel would
relish this bit of bite.

It is not my decision to make—
only a question to ponder.
I am a mere visitor to this land,
to this occurrence, to this mystery.

I will dwell on this now,
mull on it forever.

Rotorua's Ring of Fire Restaurant and Spa

Māori women bring pieces of chicken
to place on racks
above steaming sulfide black pools.
It doesn't smell good, but the meal is quickly done.
What's more, it tastes just like chicken.

Where else on earth can you watch
as handwoven flax bags full of cabbage,
purple sweet potatoes, and corn on the cob
are submerged into 161°C bubbling thermal waters?

If the luncheon kai is good,
your after treatment is even better.

Relax by slipping into a bath of liquid mud.
Smear it on your arms, your legs, your face.
Let it exfoliate those rough patches on your heels.
Lean back and look up at the bright sun-filled sky.
No worries: the mud is a natural SPF.

View the erupting geysers.
Hear their hiss and splash.
Meditate on the steaming fumaroles.
Discover the oranges, pinks, and yellows
of the minerals created.
Ease back into a warm thermal pool.
Close your eyes momentarily and enjoy.

This establishment has been rated 5 out of 5.
Comments are always welcome.

Locks of Love

There are bridges in New Zealand,
as in the States, and many other countries
that are adorned with padlocks,
of gold, of silver,
which silent public lovers gift
as locks of forever.

These locks proclaim love
between individuals, between peoples.
Thousands of them beautify bridge walks
of grace, of daily journeys.
Some have initials noted on them.
Some have names.
They secure feelings, one for another.

Passersby note their presence,
smile in unity of feeling.
The metal clasps cannot be undone.
They embrace the universal security of love.

A Binky of Hope

Knit one, purl two.
Knit one, purl two
across the row.
It's not a big blanket.
It's a baby blanket
for a newborn,
a newborn whose mother is gone,
burned by flames in the fires
sweeping across southeastern Australia.

The Blue Mountains are no longer blue.
They rise red in the morning,
glow crimson in the evening,
sending native animals racing
for their lives, their children's lives.

Like others around the world,
I cry as I knit this binky of hope
to cuddle a baby of a population
which has lost so many—
koala, kangaroo, wallaby,
bandicoot, wombat.

I send with it in the post
my love and hopes
of survival, of a bond
of unity in this our life.

About the Author

Born and raised in Chicago, Marilyn Zelke Windau lives in Sheboygan Falls, Wisconsin. Her careers have been as a middle school and elementary school art teacher, manager of the Appleton Gallery of Arts, a workshop facilitator, and a docent at John Michael Kohler Art Center. She has enjoyed painting with words since she was a teenager. Her free verse poems have appeared in many printed and online venues and anthologies. Her chapbook *Adventures in Paradise* (Finishing Line Press) and self-illustrated book of poems *Momentary Ordinary* (Pebblebrook Press) were published in 2014. Two more poetry books followed, published by Kelsay Books: *Owning Shadows* (2017) and *Hiccups Haunt Wilson Avenue* (2018).

www.ingramcontent.com/pod-product-compliance
Lightning Source LLC
Chambersburg PA
CBHW052120110526
44592CB00013B/1683